AF469146

Don't Count Your Chickens

For Louise ~ S.P.

For Gordon and Bob ~ R.C.

First published 2005 by Macmillan Children's Books
This edition published 2006 by Macmillan Children's Books
a division of Macmillan Publishers Limited
20 New Wharf Road, London N1 9RR
Basingstoke and Oxford
Associated companies throughout the world
www.panmacmillan.com

ISBN: 978-1-4050-3453-1

3 5 7 9 8 6 4 2

A CIP catalogue record for this book is available from the British Library.

Printed in Hong Kong

Don't Count Your Chickens

Written by Simon Puttock • Illustrated by Ross Collins

igloo

When Ruth-May Leghorn was six years old, her parents took her to a chicken show. Ruth-May was THRILLED! Right there and then, she knew she had to have some chickens of her own.

"Some chickens," she said, "would make me as happy as can be!"

Well, whatever Ruth-May wanted, Ruth-May usually got . . .

Ruth-May LOVED her chickens to bits.
She cuddled and she coddled them, and every morning and every night
she counted them: one! two! and she was happy.

And so were the chickens.

But one night, Ruth-May sighed and said,

"I'm tired of just two chickens ~
just two are NOT a LOT. I want more . . .
I want TWICE as many."

And since whatever Ruth-May wanted, Ruth-May usually got . . .

. . . Ruth-May got twice as many chickens to love.
She counted one, two, three, FOUR chickens
every morning and every night, and she was happy.

And so were
the chickens, mostly.

But Ruth-May was not happy for long.
"Counting four is such a bore," she sighed.
"I want MORE! I want twice as many!"

"EIGHT chickens are a LOT!"
said her mother.
"I think eight is a very nice number,"
said Ruth-May.

And since whatever Ruth-May wanted, Ruth-May usually got . . .

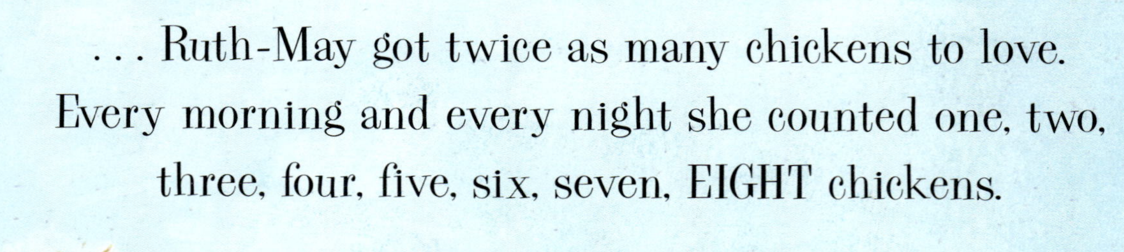

. . . Ruth-May got twice as many chickens to love. Every morning and every night she counted one, two, three, four, five, six, seven, EIGHT chickens.

And she
was happy.

But as for the chickens, they were getting
all squashed up,
and growing a mite
tetchy!

Now – did Ruth-May notice?
No, she did not! She loved her chickens, but she was too busy cuddling and coddling and counting.

And THEN guess what?

"Daddy," said Ruth-May, "what is eight and eight?"
"Ruth-May," said her father sternly, "the answer to your question is:

"NO MORE CHICKENS!"

But Ruth-May pouted, and Ruth-May sulked, and she said,
"Why, if I don't get twice as many, I shall be sad as can be."

Ruth-May's parents thought long and hard.
They did not want her to be sad as can be, so . . .

"Ruth-May," they said at last,
"tomorrow, you SHALL have
twice as many chickens."

The next day, Ruth-May got sixteen chickens to love.

And SHE was happy, but . . .

. . . the chickens were not happy AT ALL!
Those chickens were feeling cooped up and crowded in,

and fed up to the back beak with being coddled and cuddled and counted.

They decided to do something about it.

When Ruth-May went to count her chickens next morning, there was not a SINGLE ONE to count!

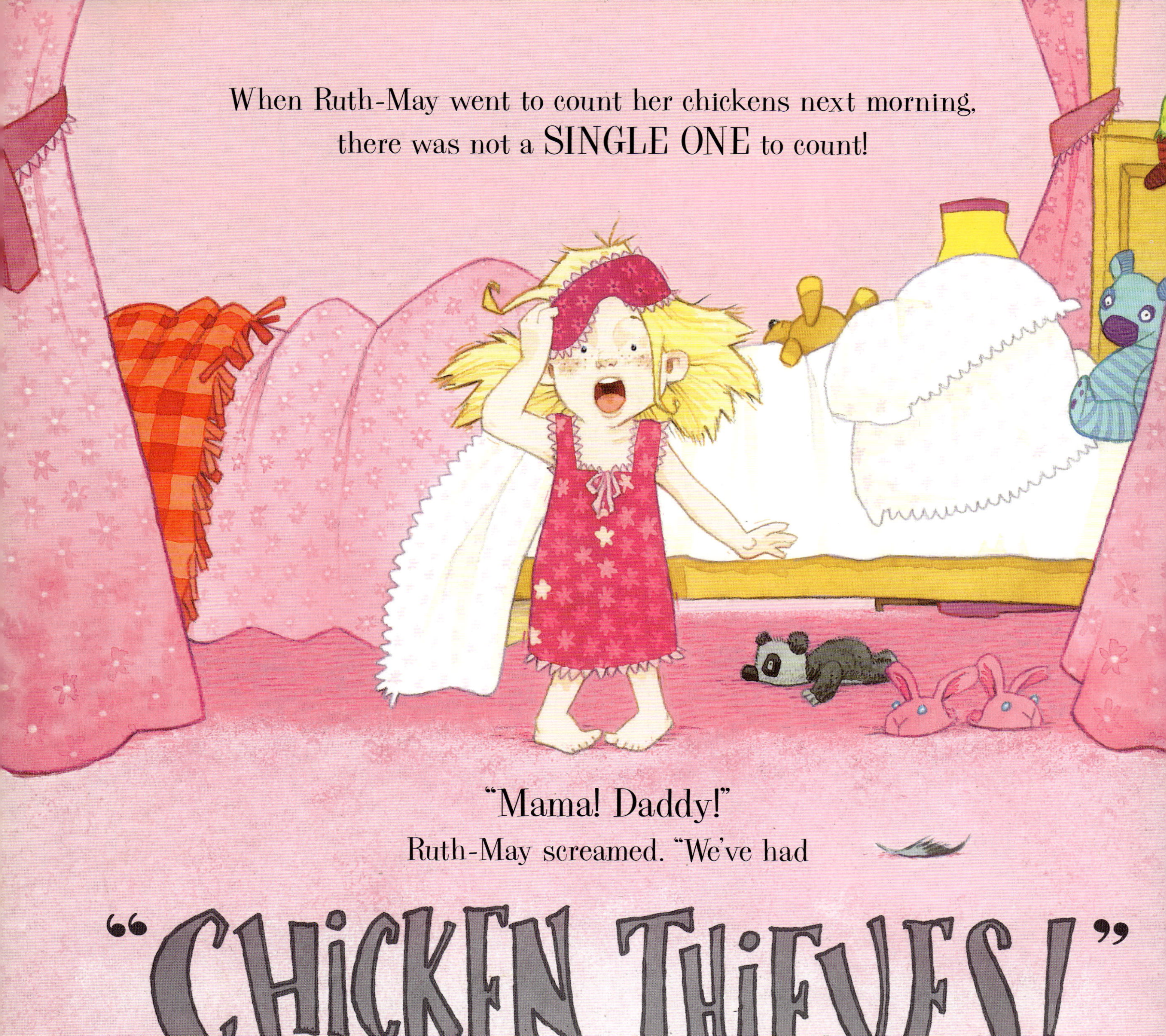

"Mama! Daddy!" Ruth-May screamed. "We've had

"CHICKEN THIEVES!"

But Ruth-May's mama and daddy said,
"Come on out to the balcony, Ruth-May, and look down yonder."

Ruth-May looked down yonder.
There, in the park, were sixteen chickens,
all scratching happily at the grass.

And in the grass were sixteen nests.

And in those nests were sixteen eggs.

"Heavens to Betsy," she cried, "there is ANOTHER way to multiply chickens! When those eggs hatch, I will have TWICE as many!"

Ruth-May's chickens had never laid EGGS before!

"Twice as many," said her daddy, "is FAR TOO MANY! Don't you think your chickens look HAPPY where they are?"

Ruth-May sighed. She had to admit that her chickens had never looked so fine, all pecking wild and free. And do you know what? Ruth-May DID NOT sulk. And she DID NOT pout.

Instead she thought long and hard.
Maybe there was ANOTHER way
to love her chickens.

"I think," she said at last,
"I'm going to leave those chickens be!"

And now, whenever Ruth-May looks down from her balcony, what does Ruth-May see?

She sees lots and lots of HAPPY chickens . . .

. . . just far TOO MANY to count!

"And that," says Ruth-May Leghorn, "makes me as HAPPY as can be!"